Little Books of Guidance
Finding answers to life's big questions!

Also in the series:
What Is Christianity? by Rowan Williams
Who Was Jesus? by James D. G. Dunn
Why Go to Church? by C. K. Robertson
How Can Anyone Read the Bible? by L. William Countryman
What Happens When We Die? by Thomas G. Long

WHAT ABOUT SEX?

A Little Book of Guidance

TOBIAS STANISLAS HALLER, BSG

Church Publishing
NEW YORK

Church Publishing
19 East 34th Street
New York, NY 10016
www.churchpublishing.org

Cover design by Jennifer Kopec, 2Pug Design
Typeset by Progressive Publishing Services

Library of Congress Cataloging-in-Publication Data

Names: Haller, Tobias Stanislas, author.
Title: What about sex? / Tobias Stanislas Haller, BSG.
Description: New York, NY : Church Publishing, [2017] |
"A Little Book of Guidance." | Includes bibliographical references.
Identifiers: LCCN 2017009371 (print) | LCCN 2017026992 (ebook) |
ISBN 9780898691368 (ebook) | ISBN 9780898691306 (pbk.)
Subjects: LCSH: Sex—Religious aspects—Anglican Communion.
Classification: LCC BT708 (ebook) | LCC BT708 .H35 2017 (print) |
DDC 241/.664—dc23
LC record available at https://lccn.loc.gov/2017009371

Printed in the United States of America

Contents

Introduction

A blushing couple in their late sixties approach the checkout at the local pharmacy, about to pay for a first Viagra prescription and a tube of lubricant. A young woman looking for a screwdriver discovers her husband's cache of pornography hidden in the garage. The parents of a teenage boy who hanged himself find his yearbook defaced with hateful epithets. A fourteen-year-old ponders which public bathroom to use while wrestling with conflicted identity.

It is all about sex.

Sex. What a powerful word! Everyone is fascinated by it, some are obsessed with it, and others wish it would just go away. Yet there it is. It is a word with double meaning: a bodily characteristic and the act through which everyone enters this world.

One goal of this book is to place sex in the context of twenty-first-century Christian life. To do so means saying something about life itself, embodied life, including that of Christ embodied in the church and in each of its members. Sex is a means by which we express love with the body. But what do we mean by *love*? Since "God is Love" and we are made in God's image, our love ought to be an expression of that image. Is that asking more of *sex* than it can bear?

This book will disappoint those looking to be told what to do. This is a book of *guidance*, not a law code. It follows Jesus's ethic of self-reflective morality: do not judge others or tell them how to live their lives, but do as you would be done by, loving your neighbor as yourself. The goal is not to lay down a law, nor to wag fingers, but to guide personal reflection on one's own life, and what Dietrich Bonhoeffer called "life together." I can offer the experience of one who has traveled the roads, pointing out difficult spots, but I won't tell you which road is best for you. I will pose questions and raise possibilities for your own exploration.

Finally, this book's Christian context is Anglican and Episcopalian, in, of, and for the twenty-first century. This means taking an approach of building on the past without burying it: making use of the tools of reason, Scripture, and tradition. Reason comes first, as Richard Hooker observed, for it exists prior to Scripture and is a "necessary instrument" without which we could not understand anything—including Scripture.[1]

Christians have applied their minds to Scripture and life, reflecting on them in many ways. Tradition is the map of that reflection. Different Christian approaches to Scripture explain the different journeys based on it. This book will emphasize the Four C's: Close reading, Context, Canon, and Culture. *Close reading* starts with the text, for careless attention to what the text *says* leads to misunderstanding what it *means*. *Context* guides understanding and applying Scripture, since it molds and conditions meaning. *Canon* relates a passage to the broader context of the whole Scripture. Finally, we consider the *cultures* within which the texts were composed, societies different from our own and each other, and realize we look at Scripture through our own cultural lenses. Culture includes the social and psychological worldview of a people's time and place, and their prejudices, expectations, knowledge, and grasp of their world. While we don't want to conform the truths of Scripture to our present culture, we don't want past cultures to hold Scripture captive, simply because those truths were first revealed in those cultures.

That is the journey before us.

Body and Soul

"If I thought I had such a thing as a soul . . . I might agree with you."

"You don't *have* a soul, Doctor. You *are* a soul. You *have* a body . . ."

—Walter M. Miller, *A Canticle for Leibowitz*

"In our world, stars are great flaming balls of gas."

"Even in your world, my son, that is not what a star is, but only what it is made of."

—C. S. Lewis, *Voyage of the Dawn Treader*

"This is Grandfather's knife. Father replaced the handle, and I replaced the blade, but this is Grandfather's knife."

—Traditional

"I wonder if I've been changed in the night? Let me think: was I the same when I got up this morning? . . . But if I'm not the same, the next question is, Who in the world am I?"

—Lewis Carroll, *Alice's Adventures in Wonderland*

Every human being—you holding this book (or tablet), I as I write these words, and every person who ever walked this earth—at one point didn't exist. Yet here we are. Each of us began with the joining of two cells: one no bigger than the period at the end of this sentence, the other a wiggle far smaller than a comma.

5

As we grew from that little punctuation, we drew substance from our mothers, and then when we came forth into the world with a cry as all mortals do, we grew from food we ate and air we breathed—material gathered from around the world, a world itself compacted of the substance of exploded stars. What a miracle that each of us can *be*, made of elements from throughout the universe and gathered against all odds to the very spots upon which I write and you read.

There are atoms in your body and mine not only once part of stars, but of other lives. Some of you and of me likely swam in fish off the coast of Alaska, grazed in herds on the Great Plains, or grew in groves of Florida or California. Like Alice in Wonderland—for our world is a place of wonder—the me and you of today are not the same me or you of yesterday or even of earlier this morning, nor will they be tomorrow. What makes up each of us is not a fixed substance but a temporary collection of stuff in constant transition.

Life goes on, but also ends—"every day a little death" as cells of our body die and are replaced moment by moment. Ultimately we will die; we will be clinically dead before then, since it takes these cells and systems working together to keep us alive. Some cells will keep on trying to work—for minutes or even hours—after hearts and brains stop.

Amazing as this is, we know this is not all there is to life. There is a you and a me—a *self*—that somehow continues to exist as we live, despite how what makes us up changes. What each of us *is*—our identity or self—isn't a fixed set of three-dimensional stuff from which we are made, but some enduring *personhood* that persists from day to day through the fourth dimension of time. Each of us is a self, an *anima*, a soul—not something you and I *have,* but what we *are.* We are embodied as a thread stringing beads together even as they are replaced. What each of us *is* is not just the current bead but the whole thread, strung through time.

Just as a musical composition is a series of sounds, each of us is a composition by God that is performed as we make choices day by day, participating in the evolving shape of the thread of melody. The cosmos, the physical world itself—including our changing bodies—is the instrument on which we collaborate with God to perform our souls. The Christian hope and faith is that this four-dimensional physical body composes a self that will persist in a risen, spiritual body, in the new creation, where we will sing in an eternal performance, joined with all the saints who have gone before, praising Christ the Lamb who is the light of the City: as in the old Appalachian hymn, "And when from death I'm free, I'll sing and joyful be, and through eternity I'll sing on."

A wise teacher said one of the great virtues is the body in the soul's care—this is a theme of this book: each of us as a soul has a body, and what we do with it has importance not just for each of us as individuals, but for all of us as human beings, and for Christians as members of the larger body of Christ. Our identity as human—made in the image of God, and thereby free to choose, "to love, to create, to reason, and to live in harmony with creation and with God"[2]—gives a persistent self to each of us, even as our bodies change. And sex—in its double meaning—is how it all starts.

Sex and Sexuality

So, what about sex? Before proceeding, a word on words is needed. My goal is to be frank but also clear. Some of the words in this conversation have multiple meanings or are used differently by other writers. For example, *sex* means both a biological quality and a sexual action. "To have sex" is ambiguous—one *has [a] sex*, but not everyone *has sex*. This is complicated by cultural differences over time and space: what is *sexual*?—a glimpse of stocking or "anything goes"?

In this book, I will use narrow definitions. *Sex* is a biological attribute, governed by genes and anatomy. It is not limited to male and female. Some use *gender* as a synonym for *sex*, but I will use *gender* for the cultural framework that categorizes acts, attitudes, emotions, or behaviors widely (but not universally) ranged from masculine to feminine. *Gender identity* is a person's self-understanding as to how they fit into their culture's gender framework, and *gender expression* is how one reveals (or conceals) a gender identity. *Sexual orientation* is one's psychological, emotional, affectional, and erotic attraction, whether acted on or not, and *sexuality* includes those sexual acts or behaviors, both mental and physical.

Each term covers a range rather than a binary either/or, and any individual will self-identify (or be identified) somewhere in a multi-dimensional web. People's gender identity may be precise or fluid, and they may express it, keep it to themselves, or express one other than what they feel. One's body can be male or female, or it can be intersex. One can have a sexuality that is active, devoted to one or many affectional or erotic partners, or one can be shy and contained as a pond on a windless day. One may find oneself attracted to persons of a different sex or gender, or one's own, or both. One can gender identify as, and express, what one's culture regards as feminine, masculine, both, or neither, regardless of one's sex. People inhabit this multidimensional matrix, but not always in the way a given culture or society expects or demands.

A Little Bible Study

You might ask, "Doesn't Genesis 1 indicate people come in two sexes, male and female?" For an answer, let's apply the tools for interpreting Scripture from the Introduction. Although many read "male and female" as adjectives in Genesis 1:27 and 5:2, the Hebrew phrase *zakar u'nqebah* consists of two indefinite *nouns*, "a male and a female." A close, contextual, and canonical reading of Genesis 1:27 shows it is not referring to *classes* of people but to two *individuals*—the first man and woman. The close reading is grammatical, discerning parts of speech. The contextual and canonical support, including succeeding chapters of Genesis, reemphasize that the original humans are conceived as a pair, the necessary actors in accounts of human origins. Genesis 2 culminates in the creation of the woman, and the formerly solitary man's recognition and acceptance of her as made of his own substance.

10

Further canonical support for this view comes from later in Genesis (6:19; 7:3, 9, 19—the only other instances in Genesis), where the indefinite noun phrase describes the *pairs* of animals to be saved in the ark. Each pair consists of "a male and a female."

This is supported by Jesus's reading of the earlier passage. In Mark 10:6–8, as in Matthew 19:4–5, the text quotes Jesus using the language of the Septuagint (a Greek translation of the Hebrew Scriptures from the second and third centuries BCE, used among Greek-speaking Jews). He refers to "the two" who become "one," his starting point for teaching the permanence of marriage.

Finally, the Damascus Document of the Qumran (Dead Sea) texts (CD 4:20–21), provides cultural evidence, citing Genesis 1:27 in a passage on marriage discipline reading "the two" as support for monogamy.

Reading these nouns as adjectives describing *categories* of people has given rise to theological speculation concerning the nature of the image of God and a defective anthropology. Sex—and sexuality, sexual orientation, and gender—is more complex than binary.

Sex: Origin and Purpose

So where does sex come from? From a Christian perspective, sex—along with everything else—comes from God. Sex is part of the created human reality—beginning in Genesis with a male and a female. But Genesis also attests to sex as a characteristic shared with other living creatures. "Be fruitful and multiply" was first addressed to birds and fish; and though Genesis 1 lacks explicit command to the land creatures, they went to work at their multiplication, providing the pairs about which Genesis speaks before the Flood. The Bible and secular science agree sex is a biological *given* common to many living creatures.

What Is Sex?

We are more than the body that makes up each of us. Because of that, easy and common (and traditional) as it is, reducing people to their sex, or taking their sex as the principal determiner of what and who they are, falls short. *Biological determinism* sees sex as the most significant thing about a person; but despite culture's shaping the church's view of sex, leading it to adopt cultural concepts of appropriate gender roles, Christianity teaches us that sex and gender are not the principal defining character of what it means to be human. Genesis 1 ("a male and a female") finds a response in Galatians ("in Christ there is no more . . . male and female").

Moreover, medicine reveals that there is more to sex than "male and female," and that gender can conflict with one's sex assigned at birth. Sex is "woven in the womb" as an emergent process. A newly fertilized ovum has sex only in chromosomal terms. The presence of the Y-chromosome indicates not that the emerging embryo *is* male but that as it grows and develops, the Y-chromosome directs the production of hormones that will (all other things being equal) induce development of male characteristics. In the womb, men and women have equivalent organs formed from the same tissues: the testes and ovaries both begin in the fetal abdomen and move to their final positions. The testes find their place outside the body cavity—but the blood vessels that feed them remain connected up just below the diaphragm. The prostate is matched by the Skene gland (now commonly called the "female prostate"—and both have functions in sexual pleasure). These body parts change shape and position as the fetus—and later the child and youth—develop. Sex is a process that continues after birth—ask anyone who has gone through puberty.

The human template is capable of being influenced by hormones generated internally at the direction of the chromosomes, and by external factors, to become male or female. But not all people are male *or* female: some have unusual configurations of chromosomes (rather than XX and XY); some possess ambiguous genitals and are assigned on that basis to a sex that doesn't match their genes or gender identity.

What Is Sex For?

"My matter is not the part of the universe I possess totally;
it is the totality of the universe I possess partially."
—Teilhard de Chardin

Sex and sexuality evolved for procreation. While some living creatures reproduce by non-sexual means, many plants and most animals reproduce by means of sexuality. But human life is about more than the creation of additional human life. And the same is true of sexuality, because not all sexuality, even in a fertile couple intent on it, can or will result in procreation. In addition to sometimes producing offspring, human sexuality can also produce pleasure and relational bonding. These are all *natural* aspects of sexuality. Any given sexual act may include all or none.

Some privilege the procreational purpose for sexuality as a matter of design. However, people spend more than the first decade of life before becoming capable of procreation, women lose that capacity after menopause, and humans (unlike most mammals) are not bound by an estrus cycle to prompt sexual engagements. So procreation is only *part* of life by design, or as I prefer, by evolution. Sex and sexuality evolved in all sexed species—most animals and many plants—to provide for genetic diversity. I raise a stronger objection if the "design" theory is applied to require that all sexuality be with the intention to procreate, and further, that it is only morally acceptable when so undertaken. The latter is the position, for example, of the Roman Catholic Church and one of the reasons for its prohibition of contraception.

However, it is not evident one can equate the *natural* (assuming one understands *nature*) with the *moral*, or the *normal* with the *normative*. What *is* is not always what *should be*. Such an equation begs the question that the *natural* has moral weight, and in this case the understanding of *nature* is less than accurate. For while sex and sexuality evolved for procreation, that is not their only use, and in themselves provide no moral guidance. The eye naturally evolved for vision, but that doesn't tell us what to see or look at. The pleasure of sexuality (given and received), and the relationships strengthened by it, are explicitly *human* purposes, and completely *natural*, given the temporary place the ability to procreate holds in a human life.

For there is more to us than our bodies, or the ability of bodies to conceive and bear more bodies. How do humans differ from other animals? One difference lies in our self-reflective consciousness, an awareness reflected in Genesis 3–4: the couple, at first not self-aware, come to conscious knowledge of themselves—symbolized by naked-ness—at the cost of losing their innocent life among wild creatures. Human self-consciousness gives rise to the ability to extend ourselves beyond the limits of our bodies by means other than procreation. It allows us to create enduring objects and ideas in addition to passing along our genes. We have long made tools—shaping the physical world to our conscious purposes—technology in the physical world, and poetry in the realm of language. *Culture* endures beyond the individual human life, in art, music, literature, and knowledge. And those who have no biological descendants can and do contribute to this fundamental human reality.

Just as being a social human contributes to the whole human reality, a couple's sexuality plays a role in building up the human qualities of their relationship, through the human capacity to love—for love of another requires both self-consciousness and awareness of another self, so that we can "love our neighbor as our self." This is reflected in Genesis 2, stressing companionship over procreation as the cause for creation of the sexes. Genesis 1 is about the human couple and their likeness to God; Genesis 2 is about the likeness of the couple to each other. The first stresses procreation and human similarity to other creatures; the second stresses the difference between the woman and the other creatures (first presented to the man as possible partners) and her similarity with the man, being made from his own substance.

So the primary question in thinking about sex and sexual-ity isn't about which body parts go where, but how the human faculty of love is played out as we make use of the bodies we have. Even the body parts have multiple uses and serve different purposes. One could take a dim view of anatomy in relation to human nature, attributed to Saint Augustine of Hippo (and others), observing, "We are born between dung and urine," or the stark judgment of Marcus Aurelius that sexuality is "just two bits of rubbing flesh and a spurt of mucus." Or we could take heart in the knowledge that human beings are made "but a little lower than the angels" and created in the image and after the likeness of God. Our selves, including our souls and bodies, allow us to participate in creation, which includes not just procreation but how our influence spreads far beyond our skin. Augustine also said, "Love God and do as you will." The question remains: How can our love and will, and the acts we perform under their influence, be morally good? And that, of course, leads to the question of what *moral* means.

Some Questions

Don't the shapes of the body parts, and how they fit together, tell us something about what they should be used for?

In a male-dominated culture, sexuality is seen in terms of penetration, which maps well to electrical plugs and sockets, but is less satisfactory in understanding human relationships. In an ideal sense, the penis fits the vagina, but the real fit of any one man and one woman may not match this ideal. The Sanskrit sexuality guide, *Kama Sutra*, describes the unsatisfactory union of a "hare" man with an "elephant" woman. Furthermore, as Robin Baker notes in his controversial 1996 *Sperm Wars*, the penis evolved its shape to thwart procreative success by rivals with access to the same female, pumping out rivals' semen. Parts of the human sexual apparatus (such as the clitoris) appear to function solely for pleasure, with no procreative purpose. The body sends mixed messages— and we are more than our bodies.

If people didn't procreate, wouldn't the human species disappear?

Yes. However, this question usually arises as a challenge to same-sexuality, with the suggestion, "If everybody did it, the human race would die out; so it must be bad." This is a seat-of-the-pants application of eighteenth-century philosopher Immanuel Kant's maxim, the categorical imperative: the duty to act in accordance with a rule you would will to see applied universally. This is not the place for in-depth analysis of Kant, but the application here is faulty. First, it doesn't correctly define *which* duties are universal. No one suggests *same-sexuality* should be universal, but that love, care, fidelity and mutuality are duties worthy of universal application. These can be realized in relationships that do not result in procreation: by same-sex couples, or infertile mixed-sex couples. Second, if procreation were a universal duty, the same categorical charge could be leveled against celibacy. I doubt those who advance this argument against same-sexuality would do so against Saint Paul, who wished (rhetorically) all were celibate (1 Cor. 7:7).

How can a man self-identify as a woman?

A small but significant number of people experience *gender dysphoria*—a deep-seated feeling that their gender identity does not match their anatomy or sex assigned at birth.

Such feelings often present themselves early in childhood: a child may reject or feel uncomfortable with the culturally accepted behaviors associated with the sex assigned at birth, or that their body somehow "isn't right." These feelings can become more intense with puberty, as body characteristics begin to develop even more out of sync with the internal sense of identity. Gender dysphoria can be addressed through options including psychological and psychiatric counseling (primarily to deal with associated depression and anxiety), behavioral adaptation (adopting some of the gender expressions that match the gender identity), hormone blockers prescribed at the onset of puberty or gender-affirming hormones prescribed later in life, and a range of surgical procedures that can remodel the body in ways that affirm the individual's gender identity. These forms of transition can help to reduce the dysphoria and relieve the accompanying distress, anxiety, and depression.

Aren't transgender people just gay?

Sexual orientation and gender identity are different, and there is a spectrum within each. A transgender person *might* also have a same-sexual orientation, either before or after transition. However, many (though not all) trans people wish to adopt the cultural conventions associated with their gender identity—from the restroom they use to whom they wish to marry—and would not think of themselves as having a same-sexual orientation.

Setting the Moral Compass

Christianity, like most religious traditions, recognizes a difference between *is* and *ought*. This is the territory of *morality* or *ethics* and to navigate it one uses a "moral compass." One purpose of this book is to help provide such guidance, rather than a list of dos and don'ts. There are, of course, many different systems of ethics or morality, even within the Christian tradition.

Directions Not Taken

Here are three moral approaches less helpful in a twenty-first-century Christian context.

Natural Law

This moral system was given classic exposition by Thomas Aquinas. It dominated Christian thinking for centuries, despite its flaws, the principal of which is a form of circular reasoning. Natural law holds "moral duties can be ascertained by reflection on human nature."[3] But this presumes there is a universal "human nature" that always seeks and desires the same goals and ignores the influence of culture. (Within Western Christianity it also runs into the difficulty of discerning what is moral from an assumedly *fallen* human nature.) There may be a limited number of goals shared by all humans, regardless of culture, but it is a further leap to accept these ends as *good*, or to hold anything obstructing them as *evil*. For example, natural law argues that because life is a goal of human existence, the reproduction of human life is a good that must not be thwarted by contraception and that separating sexuality from conception is a moral wrong. This fails to account for alternative views that take account of the *quality* of life rather than life itself as an absolute good, or the fact that sexuality does not always lead to conception even when nothing is done to prevent it. In the long run, what people *are* by nature (if that can be determined) is no indicator of what they *should be*. And cultural notions of what people *should be* may be read into human nature rather than from it.

Asceticism

This ethic views pleasure with suspicion if not condemnation, at its most extreme with some of the anti-material attitudes of Gnostic and Manichaean philosophy. Augustine of Hippo has been credited with weaving this strand into Christianity, but the connection of pleasure—especially sexual pleasure— with sin was present in Christian thinking much earlier, particularly in monastic circles or those influenced by Stoicism. By Augustine's time it was widely held that every sexual act—even between a married couple—partook of the nature of sin and that pleasure itself was proof sin was present. This view takes pleasure as suspicious and guilty, and takes suffering (the opposite of pleasure) as expiatory—but it begs the question by assuming there is something wrong with pleasure, something that requires punishment.

Hedonism

The pleasure principle has rarely found a home in Christian thinking—largely due to the strength of asceticism—but has been a part of secular thought in many times and places, from the reflections of philosopher Jeremy Bentham to the swinging sixties, "If it feels good, do it." This opposite of asceticism casts pleasure as the primary determiner of what is good. The obvious problem with this approach lies in the question, "Whose pleasure?" Is it the utilitarian "greatest good for the greatest number" even if that means suffering for the few? Why should pleasure or pain in themselves be given any moral weight at all? An ascetic who stubs a toe may feel virtuous for enduring the pain, while a hedonist may feel virtuous for skill in discerning a fine wine.

If we are to find a basis for a Christian ethic—including a sexual ethic—we must look deeper.

Sexuality and the Bible

To find a more explicitly Christian ethic for sexuality, we look to Scripture as a primary source. Here we face a problem, for the Bible doesn't say a great deal about sexuality, and much of what it says is inconsistent. Things allowed in one part of Scripture are proscribed in another, things are allowed or mandated in Scripture that are considered serious crimes in much of today's world, and some things forbidden in biblical law today barely raise an eyebrow. This should come as no surprise, because the texts that comprise the Bible come from a wide span of time and several different cultures—all different from our own.

These differences are most obvious in the Hebrew Scriptures. The first thing we note regarding sexual regulations is *asymmetry*: rules are not applied equally to men and women. For example, under Hebrew law, a married man could have relationships with prostitutes, form a regular bond with a concubine, or have additional wives, without incurring a charge of adultery. A married woman, however, was bound to her sole husband, expected to be a virgin until married (Deut. 22:20–21). Under Hebrew scriptural law, a man could only commit adultery against another man, a woman only against her husband.

This view stems from how the Hebrew authors thought about sexuality and about what constituted marriage. Most simply, sexuality was something men *did*—a male *thing*, in a literal sense: the phallus and what a man did with it constituted sexuality. Women were *vessels* that receive a man's input, figuratively as a field receives seed—and it is no accident that *semen* is literally "seed" in all of the biblical languages (and in the Latin root of the English word.) Marriage was a process by which a man *took* possession of a woman almost as real estate.

Even the biblical law against male same-sexuality was cast in terms of what men did to women: "With a male do not lay the layings of a woman" (Lev. 18:22). This is also one reason the Hebrew Scripture is silent on female same-sex relationships. As the later rabbis observed, from a phallic perspective, two women couldn't have intercourse because they lack the necessary equipment.[4]

Some of these views and laws on sexuality changed by the time of Christ and the apostolic church of the New

Testament, not only in the Jewish world, but also in Greek and Roman cultures. Although Roman law identified adultery as one man's crime against another man's marriage or a woman's against her own, and although it allowed men free access to prostitutes and mistresses (though taking a firm stand on monogamy), Roman and Greek moralists had begun to see prostitution as unvirtuous. Jewish teachers, including the later prophets and the writers of the Second Temple era, adopted a similar moral attitude. Vice lists from the New Testament and Apostolic/Patristic eras begin to pair prostitution and adultery (*porneia* and *moixeia*), putting men and women on more equal footing (see Matt. 15:19, some manuscripts of Mark 7:21, and Barnabas 19:4). This is an outgrowth of the legal situation: since a married man could only commit adultery with another man's wife, any *un*married woman he bedded could be considered a harlot (*zonah, porne*—though Roman law allowed a married man a concubine not considered a prostitute.) Early Christian writers followed Jesus in adopting the stricter view. For example, at the turn of the fourth century Lactantius counters the civil law of his time, extending the definition of adultery to men and woman equally (*Divine Institutes* 6.23).

Similarly, from the positive side, Jewish and Christian biblical writers, especially Paul, placed marital relations in greater balance and mutuality, emphasizing fidelity and permanence. This trend continued in the early church.

As to things once mandated but now disallowed, and once forbidden but now tolerated, I will give one example of each. The "levirate law" (Deut. 25:5ff) enjoins a man to marry his brother's childless widow, begetting children in his brother's name. This was longstanding practice (see Gen. 38:8ff); the custom appears in several other places, including the story of Ruth and in the Sadducees' confrontation with Jesus (Luke 20:28ff). The early church, emphasizing monogamy and recognizing the inconsistency of the levirate law with the incest regulations forbidding relations with a sister-in-law (Lev. 18:16), outlawed the practice. This touches Anglicans and Episcopalians: a papal dispensation allowed Henry Tudor to marry his childless brother Arthur's widow, Catherine of Aragon—we know how well that worked out, as the pope refused to reverse the dispensation when Henry appealed to Leviticus.

For an example of something condemned in Scripture but now barely mentioned, consider this sexual regulation: "You shall not approach a woman to uncover her nakedness while she is in her menstrual uncleanness" (Lev. 18:19). This prohibition continued in the early church (the Constitutions of the Holy Apostles, a late fourth-century work, classed it with pederasty and adultery.) In time, this "biblical crime" faded from the law-books. (Some argue Roman Catholic permission for natural family planning—the "rhythm method"—expressly *allows* intercourse during at least part of the menstrual cycle.[5])

None of this means Scripture doesn't allow us to frame a moral approach, or help set a moral compass. But to do so we should move away from treating Scripture as an answer-book, looking instead to the principles underlying the specifics derived from particular world-views and understandings of human nature. In all journeys, cultural geography shapes how one travels: when faced by a lake or mountain one may not be able to head due north—culture influences how one applies a moral compass.

The Jesus Ethic

Groundwork for an ethical system emerges within Scripture, one that—for Christians—crystalizes in the teaching of Jesus, a Jew who participated in the evolving ethics of rabbinic Judaism. Jesus provides a basis for our moral compass: not a law-code with a list of precise dos and don'ts, but a general rule, a reflective way of looking critically at ourselves (and at others only with forgiveness). This "Jesus Ethic" has several characteristics, each with implications for sexuality—as for all of life.

He focuses on the Decalogue and the two commandments in the "Summary of the Law" when citing Torah.

A good example is his response when asked what one must do to have eternal life. Jesus cites a subset of the Ten Commandments (Luke 18:20; Mark 10:19), appending the law of love of neighbor (Matt. 19:18–19 quoting Lev. 19:18, the only quote from Leviticus in Jesus's teaching). Love of neighbor, paired with honoring God with one's whole being (Deut. 6:5) is the basis for "the law and the prophets" (Matt. 22:40). Earlier in Matthew (7:12) Jesus assigns this quality to the Golden Rule.

Two of the Ten Commandments have sexual content. "You shall not commit adultery" and "You shall not covet . . . your neighbor's wife" (Exod. 20:14, 17). While the Hebrew understanding of adultery focused on male privilege, and the law regulating desire for another's possessions similarly focused on male aspirations, Jesus applies them more universally, reflecting on the importance of fidelity and avoidance of misplaced desire.

He intensifies morality not in severity but direction: internally.

While Jesus recognizes the whole of the law even as he fulfills it (Matt. 5:18; Luke 16:17), his approach is to summarize and internalize. He builds on the Tenth Commandment and fixes the moral compass in the heart's intentions. The wrong in murder is anger (Matt. 5:21–22), and adultery begins with desire (5:27–28). This implies that sexual morality is not just about things done, but contemplated even if left undone. In dismissing the dietary law Jesus affirms the source of defilement is the corrupted heart (Mark 7:22–23).

He applies morality equally to men and women.

Jesus extends "adultery" to men and women equally (Matt. 5:27–28, 19:9; Luke 16:18). This may explain his reaction to "the woman taken in the act of adultery" (John 8:3). The absent man with whom she was discovered would equally have been subject to the death penalty. Jesus forestalls any notion of particular male or female sexual vices or virtues.

He builds on the prophets and their insights and discounts the dietary and ceremonial law.

Jesus joins the prophets in emphasizing justice, fairness, generosity, and fidelity—concepts present in the Torah, but renewed by prophets such as Micah (6:11). Jesus joins Malachi (2:14–16) in deprecating divorce. He rejects the dietary law, and internalizes the ceremonial law, stressing the Sabbath as time for doing good (Matthew 12:12), and true worship as spiritual and embodied in works of mercy, rather than ceremony or sacrifice (John 4:21–23; Matt. 9:13). The application to sex turns from emphasis on anatomy to focus on loving, just, and merciful actions. (Luke 11:27–28)

In framing the Golden Rule, he stresses the positive, and "the other."

Jesus's ethic may be called *Gospel altruism.* "Do unto others as you would have them do to you" demands subjective positive generosity, the choice for the other rather than the self. It adds a prophetic, positive edge to the negative formulations about *not* doing to others as one would not be done by. Some think this rule's subjectivity implies moral relativism, but Jesus affirms that righteousness cannot reside in an absolute list of actions declared always to be right or wrong; actors, circumstances, situations, and above all intentions must be considered, directed by a moral compass guiding toward doing for others what one would want done to oneself, even at cost to oneself. When the rich young man asks Jesus about inheriting eternal life (Matt.19:16ff), Jesus cites obedience to the divine commandments, adding the love of neighbor as oneself. When the man says he has done all this, Jesus says perfection will be found in devoting his wealth to the poor and dedicating himself as a disciple. Only self-offering can perfectly save the self. In the Gospel altruism of Jesus, to lose is the only way to win—to lose this world for the sake of the next (John 12:25). There is no greater love than self-sacrifice for others (John 15:13).

Another critique of this rule is that it might permit one to harm others if one were content to be harmed oneself. Yet I may not force what I like on others *who do not like it*, for I would not want anything that *dis*pleases me to be done to me. Consent is crucial, and "no" means *no*. Any action that violates another's person or personhood cannot be in keeping with the Golden Rule.

Jesus embodies the ethic of one who came to serve, not to be served, and to give his life (Matthew 20:28). The Golden Rule is altruistic, self-giving: there is no recompense in this formula, any payback is subjunctive—what you *would* want done. One invites the poor to dinner precisely because they are not able to reciprocate (Luke 14:14). The end or goal of virtue is in the act itself. There is, of course, a reward for virtue, but it resides in the ultimate end of humanity, why humanity exists: to glorify and enjoy God.

This has implications for sexuality. Genesis (1:27) tells us humanity came into existence as the earthly image of the transcendent God. The transitory purpose was to fill the earth and subdue it (28). But as Augustine put it (*On the Trinity* 8), the final purpose of humanity is contemplation of God, the perfect altruist. God is all gift, without any need at all. As "no one has seen God" in this world, God gives us each other as images of God—children of God, siblings of each other—to practice on. We learn to love God by loving each other, as God loves us, altruistically (1 John 4:12). As creatures, humans have needs, but the image of God shines through human beings when they give themselves to others, one's abundance supplying another's need, bearing one another's burdens in a shared life. In sexuality, this is embodied not in the objectifying *use of* each other but the mutual *gift* of each *to* the other. We treat other human beings as ends in themselves (not means to other ends) because they are the earthly embodiment of the image of God, our final end. The ethic of Jesus calls me not to transform a person into a tool for achieving my own ends, but to see my relationship with that person as the embodiment of the true end toward which human *being* is called.

He limits judgment to self-judgment.

Jesus rejects judging others but urges forgiving harm done to oneself (Matt. 7:1; Luke 6:37); one can be as tough on oneself as possible, because only the individual (and God) know what is within one's heart. (Matt. 5:29–30; 18:8–9) He emphasizes duty and responsibility, in a community in which none is to rule over others. The goal is fraternal service rather than paternalistic rule (Luke 22:26) for all have "one Father in heaven" (Matt. 23:9; John 13:13–14). This means two things: an eye upon one's own conscience, imagination, and actions; and suspending judgment of others.

These are the characteristics of the moral compass Jesus provides: not a law code, but guiding principles. Any choice you make about the exercise of your sexuality, and any other action, ought to be guided by the compass that points to love.

Love in Action

When I speak of love as the pole of the moral compass, I do not mean *romantic love*. Romance and emotion have a part in human life, perhaps most especially in how we express our sexuality. But *moral* love is about more than emotion or disposition; love is an *act* to will the best for the beloved, even to loss of oneself. It is not about self-gratification but about willing good to others.

As the soul gives meaning to the body, love gives meaning to sexuality. These meanings go by various names by which love is known: desire, affection, and friendship. The different loves can combine and overlap. A couple may have a powerful erotic connection as well as a warm friendship; but one may have deep friendships without eroticism. Think of life as a house: the bedroom is only one room, and has more than one function. Love makes a house a home, in part because it threads the life of those who dwell in it through all the rooms.

Sexuality expresses love when exercised for the good of the other. That does not mean it cannot also please the one expressing it; that is one of the wonderful things about sexual love—it can be mutually joyful. When selfishness enters in, the relationship becomes unbalanced, even transactional.

The question is: How do I apply this moral compass to how I express love with my body, including my sexuality?

Acts and Relationships

We've described Jesus's moral compass, and we have begun to look at how to apply it to the acts and relationships through which we express sexuality and love for others—how we determine what acts and relationships are right for us. Let's examine some specifics, apply the Scripture and the compass, and look at the questions raised.

Before beginning, I want to eliminate directions toward which the moral compass does *not* point, by their very nature, because they depend on a lack of consent, or on duplicity: rape and infidelity. The interest here is in choices to act and relate which have been, or are beginning to be, seen as *capable* of being moral. Those choices will be yours, judging for yourself, not others.

Casual Sexuality

There is nothing new about casual sexuality, without commitment, with single or multiple partners. But casual sexuality is not without consequences—beyond unintended pregnancy.

Biblical commentary on casual sexuality is mixed, though there is an arc that bends away from the casual to the committed. A Hebrew man could visit prostitutes without breaking the law; and "neither the Scriptures nor the rabbinical authorities forbade simple noncommercial fornication between consenting partners"[6]—but fathers were forbidden to prostitute their daughters (Lev. 19:29) and a man who seduced a woman not already engaged was to marry her if her father consented, or pay a dowry if he refused—her lost virginity limiting her future marital options (Exod. 22:16–17). The negative view of fornication (*porneia* as commercial prostitution or casual sexuality without the *intention* of marriage) is well in place by the Christian era, in part perhaps due to being linked with idolatry (for which it long served metaphorically).

Prostitution itself is less casual in that it commercializes sexuality. Is the commercialization of sexuality in prostitution more demeaning to the prostitute than the commercialization of food in a restaurant is to a chef? Even when prostitution is regulated and the safety and health of sex workers is protected, is there an element of coercion that violates the moral compass? Is the *use* of another human being for one's own satisfaction capable of building up? On the other hand, what if the prostitute finds this a means to personal self-realization, or the relationship is mutually satisfying even if commercial? What if rather than being casual, the relationship is long-lasting and fully consensual?

In noncommercial casual sexuality, can something so intimate really be entirely *casual*? Or does it naturally create connection, as Paul says, when a man unites with a woman even though no commitment is intended (1 Cor. 6:16)? Can "friends with benefits" truly remain friends and treat sexuality as no more than dinner and a movie? Considering the rejection of hedonism, is "if it feels good do it" a sufficient guide? Is "no strings" a viable moral option?

Premarital Sexuality

The "modern" ideal was that a husband and wife would arrive at the altar rail as virgins and have their first sexual encounter on their wedding night. This ideal applied asymmetrically in most cultures where Judaism and Christianity flourished; men might have sexual experience before marriage, but bridal virginity was expected (or demanded, Deut. 22:20). The idea of marriage as a ceremonial act, prior to which a couple is forbidden sexual relations, is not clearly expressed in Scripture. Through the complex legal history of marriage in Jewish and much Christian tradition, if a couple intended marriage (expressed by betrothal or "future consent"—*consensus per verba de futuro*) such sexuality wasn't *premarital* but effected the marriage.

Betrothal gave way to *engagement,* and that is often less formal than it was even a few decades ago. It is widely accepted that couples will have had sexual experience together prior to marriage. Instead of forming the idealized crowning achievement that seals the marriage, many now expect or accept it even prior to engagement.

There is a distinction, however, between *casual* and *premarital* sexuality: the intention of the couple. So, what is the intent? Is it to make this person the one, lifelong partner? *Premarital* is necessarily related to *marital*: as casual sexuality increases, does *premarital* ultimately only apply to the final partner in a series?

Auto-eroticism

Auto-eroticism (masturbation) is the most casual of all casual sexuality, but as common as it is, it has been judged at times to be a serious failing. Such judgments should be set against the moral compass to determine their accuracy. Scripture makes no mention of it—Onan's fate (Gen. 38:9) stems from his failure to obey the custom (before it became part of the Mosaic law) to impregnate his brother's childless widow. On the "natural law" view, tradition has been negative, at times regarding masturbation as grave, at others dismissing it—particularly among the young—as a fault to be avoided. Science provides minimal guidance, noting that male masturbation may rid a man of aging and unhealthy sperm, and assist with the treatment of such ailments as nonbacterial inflammation of the prostate.[7] Finally, popular culture provides a range of epithets to portray it as a common weakness.

The moral compass raises important questions: Isn't self-gratification selfish? Is the pleasure derived from such actions wrong, as some think, because—like sexual acts with birth control, or same-sex sexuality—the pleasure is separated from a purported *end*? Is pleasure without one productive object among others wrong? For instance, is it morally wrong for one to enjoy the scent of a flower, or the beauty of a sunset, even though it leads to no end other than the sensation itself? When accompanied by fantasy or pornography, does masturbation overlap with what Jesus said about adultery (Matt. 5:28)? How does the Golden Rule apply to a solitary act, except to the extent it might selfishly interfere with or replace one's relationship(s)? Only a careful self-examination can address this most subjective form of sexuality.

Pornography

Pornography raises moral questions in both production and use. By commercializing sexuality, it transforms relationship into commodity, as in prostitution. It is difficult to reconcile this transformation with the Golden Rule. Do those who model or perform in pornography do so as free agents, or are they to some extent coerced, even if only by financial enticements? Do those who use pornography for sexual stimulation do so to support their own loving relationships, or does the pornography become a substitute? To what extent do the models or performers make one less appreciative of one's own perhaps less glamorous spouse or partner?

Same-Sexuality

A bibliography on same-sexuality would be longer than this book.[8] As with much else, social and religious attitudes include selective negativity, outright condemnation, limited toleration, and full acceptance—including civil and religious marriage.

Scripture offers uneven testimony: the claim that the Bible "condemns homosexuality" in all forms and situations, is unsupported by the text. For example, there is no mention of same-sexuality between women in the Hebrew Scripture. And the single New Testament verse alleged to forbid such sexuality (Rom. 1:26) is neither a specific commandment, nor clearly referring to women engaged in sexual acts with each other—it may refer to women allowing their husbands to use them for anal intercourse, "exchanging the natural use for that which is unnatural" and so "in the same way" leading the men to do *the same* with each other. Some early writers understood the text in this way, including Clement of Alexandria (*Instructor* II.87.1) and Augustine of Hippo (*On Marriage and Concupiscence* 2.20, *The Good of Marriage* 12), though others, such as John Chrysostom, read it as applying to lesbianism (Homily IV on Romans).

A handful of verses judge male same-sexuality negatively. A close, contextual, and cultural reading shows these texts may refer either to rape, incest, prostitution, or idolatry. The story of Sodom (Gen. 19:4–11) concerns the threat of gang-rape. The principal legal prohibition on male same-sexuality in the holiness law-code (Lev. 18:22; 20:13) condemns a male who beds a male as a woman, or allows himself so to be treated. It may reflect the incest rules of the immediate context (that is, to avoid bedding a male with the "beddings of a woman" within the family degrees of the preceding verses); or it may reflect concerns about idolatry and pagan prostitution, tagged by the word *abomination* (*toevah*). In any case, it is not a universal commandment for all times, places, and peoples, but it restricts Israelites (and resident aliens) in the land of Israel (Lev.18:26).[9]

Some argue Paul has this law in mind by reference to *arsenokoitai* in 1 Corinthians 6:9 (with *malakoi*—perhaps a passive partner, youth or prostitute; or a "wanker," or someone literally "weak" or "soft") and 1 Timothy 1:10, but his attitude is likely formed by the sorts of male same-sexuality he might have encountered in a Graeco-Roman context: pederasty and prostitution. (Long-term, mutual, same-sex relations in this cultural context were rare, and as Aristophanes' sarcasm in Plato's *Symposium* indicates, considered absurd, if not scandalous. The Greco-Roman culture accepted pederasty and prostitution, but an adult "passive" male partner was subject to ridicule.) A canonical and culturally informed reading that includes the passage from Romans 1:22–32—describing the orgiastic behavior of idol-worshipers, real or imagined—provides a hint of the lens through which Paul sees. He condemns what pagans approve, with no need for him to condemn what they already hold contemptible.

There is a danger in reading Romans 1 as primarily about same-sexuality, missing Paul's main thesis. He condemns the gentiles for worshiping creation rather than the Creator—not for *departing* from some "created order" but for *exchanging* God for idols as the object of worship. This leads them to do things they ought not, including the orgies of the mystery cults (as Paul imagined them)—something far from modern notions of life-long, adult same-sex relationships, including marriage. Yet in our context, those negative toward such relationships often place creation on a pedestal, arguing that there is something in the sex-difference ("complementarity") that renders it capable of holiness, or reflecting the divine image or the Trinity. Ironically, the earlier Christian disdain for sexuality, as part of our "lower" animal nature, has in recent years given way to idealization even of the bodily anatomy of male and female as somehow revelatory. This is a form of putting "confidence in the flesh" (Phil. 3:3)—exaltation of body parts and how they interact—rather than in the spiritual values of love, fidelity, and care that human flesh can express through the human agency that animates it.

Some allege that while one might mitigate the texts cited *against* same-sexuality, there is nothing in Scripture to commend it. This overlooks (or dismisses) the greatest love story in Scripture—that of Jonathan and David. Let's apply a close, contextual, canonical, and cultural reading to the account (1 and 2 Samuel beginning at chapter 18).

Some say reading this as a love story confuses friendship with love. First, the text provides a response: the Hebrew word for "friend" (*re'ah*) is not used to describe Jonathan and David's relationship. (The term *is* later used of David's friend Hushai, 2 Sam. 15:37; 16:16, 17.) On the contrary, the text says, "Jonathan *loved* David," not as a friend but "as his own soul," as *soul-mates* "knit together" (1 Sam. 18:1). Second, this is a case of "love at first sight"—and while love at first sight is real, no one ever heard of friendship at first sight. (Jeremy Bentham noted this around the end of the eighteenth century, in *Not Paul but Jesus*.) Third, Jonathan immediately makes "a covenant with him in his love for him as his own soul" (18:3). This covenant, and the form it takes—Jonathan strips himself of his clothing and arms (18:4)—has sometimes been read as a pledge of same-sex love. These opening verses of chapter 18 are missing from some Greek versions of the Bible, which may indicate they were absent from some of the underlying Hebrew texts. Finally, as C. S. Lewis observed in *The Four Loves*, "Lovers are normally face to face, absorbed in each other; Friends, side by side, absorbed in some common interest." The story of Jonathan's love for David lacks "common interest" and reveals total absorption of Jonathan with David, their souls knit together in and by love.

As with any romance, there is conflict. Jonathan's father Saul was already *taken with* David (1 Sam. 16:21; and then *took* him from his father's house—18:2). David is one of few biblical characters described as a physical beauty; his name means "Beloved" and he is the love-interest of several characters in the account, which takes a tragic turn in part due to the rivalry of father and son for David's love. This explains Saul's telling curse aimed at his son: "You have *chosen* the son of Jesse to your own shame, and to the shame of your mother's nakedness" (1 Sam. 20:30). Leviticus 18:7 suggests this may be Saul's oblique reference to his own relationship with David, since the nakedness of mother and father are equivalent. Although Saul recognized David as a threat to Jonathan's royal accession (1 Sam. 20:31), there is more at work than dynastic anxiety (an anxiety totally lacking on Jonathan's part, as their final woodland tryst, 1 Sam. 23:16–18, shows).

Another common objection is that the text lacks explicit eroticism between Jonathan and David. First, Hebrew Scripture is reticent when it comes to sexuality. Euphemisms abound: sexuality is rendered with to *know*, to *take* and to *lie with*, and the more direct to *go into* (Gen. 4:1; 34:2; 29:23). Body parts lack explicit names: males have *flesh* or *feet* (Exod. 28:42; 4:25) and women *foreheads* or perhaps *sockets* (Isa. 3:17). Given this tendency to euphemism, we should not expect an X-rated account. What there is in the texts concerning Jonathan and David is deeply emotional, with embraces and tears. The incident most likely euphemizing a sexual encounter is in 1 Samuel 20. Modern translations such as the NRSV downplay the romantic Hebrew: "I have found favor in your eyes" becomes "you like me" (20:3). During planning how to notify David of Saul's intentions, Jonathan breaks off conversation with, "Come, let us go into the field." This same phrase appears in the erotic Song of Songs (7:11), which commentator Martin Pope connects with pre-Israelite sacred marriage imagery, "as innocent or as suggestive as one may wish to make it."[10] In David and Jonathan's case, what follows is renewal of their "love covenant" (17) and planning for the elaborate scheme to alert David of Saul's intent. Later, the whole point of this plan is abandoned, as the two cannot bear to part without a face-to-face encounter. David rises from his hiding place, falls to the ground before Jonathan, and the two weep and kiss and embrace and . . . Well, here the text is cryptic: the Hebrew says, "*ad dawid higdil*" = "until David enlarged" (41). This is usually understood to mean that David wept more than Jonathan, but it may be a euphemism, or a rare alternate meaning for *higdil* as "wove together." Acknowledging that there are male same-sexual acts that do not involve penetration, at the end of this encounter, replete with falling to the ground, embracing, kissing, and weeping, Jonathan states that their pledge is now between his and David's "seed"—a word that enjoys all the connotations with which euphemism can supply it. There is no question this is a love scene. Whether it includes sexuality is veiled in discretion.

A final objection is that David and Jonathan are fathers of children, and David is portrayed throughout as a ladies' man. First, many men marry or court women, from convention or social pressure, regardless of their sexual orientation—including those attracted to both sexes. Second, the primary romantic impetus comes from Jonathan; David may have reciprocated—at the end lamenting the death of Jonathan as "greatly beloved," whose love "was wonderful, passing the love of women" (2 Sam. 1:24). This verse ought to be taken for what it says, which was clear enough to Jerome that he bowdlerized it in his Latin translation by adding "as a mother loves her only son, so I loved you." Did David truly love Jonathan? Or was this the act of the clever politician the rest of the account reveals, expounding a public lament for the deceased members of the dynasty he supplanted? This much is clear, Jonathan loved David with a love that was true to the point of loving him as his whole self (soul, mind, and body, as the Hebrew *nephesh* includes them all) and to risk all he had and knew for his sake, including his life. In this, the love of Jonathan for David fulfills the law of loving one's neighbor as oneself, and it echoes both "the greatest love" of John 15:13 and the marital love of Ephesians 5:33.

In conclusion, Scripture itself does not answer how one ought to consider same-sex relationships. Those portrayed negatively can be understood to apply to rape, incest, prostitution, or idolatry; and as the greatest love story in Scripture portrays a same-sex love—even if not consummated—the best course is for everyone to apply the moral compass the same way, guiding their lives in mixed- or same-sex relationships toward love. Good resides in how people treat each other, not in the genital plumbing they have.

Polyamory/Polygamy

This may be defined as having more than one sexual partner or spouse, with all involved consenting to the arrangement, whether one-to-many or in a more complex agreement. There have been contexts in which one man having multiple partners (or spouses) *without* such consent was not only possible but permitted. Under Torah law, a man did not need his wife's approval or consent to take a second wife, and children born into polygamous marriages had rights (Deut. 21:15). (Given the asymmetrical sex roles in Jewish law, women were restricted to one husband.) Polygamous marriages could be loving and caring, but they also opened the door to rivalry: both aspects are illustrated in the household of Samuel's father Elkanah, and his wives Hannah and Penninah (1 Sam.1:1–8).

Polygamy was not permitted under Roman law (though polyamory through concubinage was possible and common) and monogamy became an ideal in Christian and sectarian Jewish circles; Jesus (Matt. 19:5–6) and the Qumran community (Damascus Document 4:20–21) both cite Genesis as the basis for permanent, exclusive monogamy; and the Pastoral Epistles call for clergy to have one wife (1 Tim. 3:2, 12; Titus 1:6 limits a cleric to one wife in a lifetime, disallowing remarriage should a wife die). A similar rule is laid down for "true" widows (1 Tim. 5:9).

Given the state of civil law today, polygamy remains rare, and in most places it exists all parties must consent to the arrangement. Arguments in polygamy's favor are sometimes advanced, and polyamory—as a formalized (if not legally recognized) stable, consensual relationship among three or more persons—has been advocated by some.

Applying the moral compass raises questions. Given the reality of envy, jealousy, and pride, are polyamorous relationships subject to the sorts of problems Scripture attests befell polygamous marriages? Is consent from every party in the relationship entirely free from pressure? (Note that these same questions can be asked of monogamous marriages in a social context!) Given the multiple valences, can the dynamics of the more complex relationships be mutual and reciprocal? Is there a substantive difference between "each other" and "one another," *between* a couple and *among* members of a group?

Celibacy

It might seem odd to mention celibacy in a discussion of sexuality, but it belongs in the larger context of what one does with one's sexual reality. Even if one renounces sexuality, there is no escaping sex, sexual orientation, gender, and gender identity and expression. Celibacy—understood both as being *unmarried* and *abstinent* from active sexuality—is as subject to ethical standards as sexual activity. As Paul wrote in Romans 14 concerning observances of diet and day, all stand under the judgment of God but are called to judge their own lives set against the moral compass of the love of God. If celibacy is approached as a kind of Aristotelian egoism—merely to be virtuous from an ascetic point of view—it hardly jibes with the Gospel value of altruism. If the celibate merely internalizes sexual impulses and allows them free rein in fantasy, she falls short of Jesus's standard. Has the celibate made this choice to avoid or suppress her own sexuality in order to be of service to others, free from responsibilities to a spouse so as to serve the church? Celibacy has been cast as a form of Christian marriage, in which the celibate is married to the Lord—sometimes explicitly so with a wedding band. The impulse to celibacy can arise from fear—but also from love.

Marital Sexuality

Marriage[11] has long been considered the ideal context for sexuality. At the same time, marriage does not guarantee all sexuality taking place within it is directed by the moral compass. Bad and abusive marriages exist—and coercion is as much a violation within marriage as without; even more, because it betrays a vow. Married couples are no less responsible to frame their sexual lives by the moral compass than the unmarried.

Scripture on Marriage and Sex

In the Hebrew Scriptures, the dominant understanding of marriage is unequal: the man rules over a woman (or several women), and has access to other unmarried women. A man can gain a wife by seduction, conquest, inheritance, or as her father's gift (Exod. 22:16; Deut. 21:10–14; Deut. 25:5ff; Gen. 29:18ff). Inequality is embedded in marriage language: the husband is "lord" (*baal*) of the woman; a married woman is "governed" (*beulah*) or "has a lord/master" (*beulat baal*). This inequality was regarded as derived from the curse on Eve: "He shall rule over you" (Gen. 3:16).

But it was not so in the beginning, when Adam recognized equality in his joy encountering Eve—one like himself; taken (as Jews and Christians interpreted) from his side to stand beside, rather than from his head or his foot to rule or to be ruled (Gen. 2:23).

In a prophetic promise, Hosea (2:16) recognized a restored balance, portraying a loving husband—God speaking to an unfaithful but redeemed spouse—Israel: "On that day, says

44

the Lord, you will call me, 'My husband,' and no longer will you call me, 'My Baal.'" This prophetic return to the *ish* and *ishah*, husband and wife, of Eden expresses their fundamental equality, as God intended.

The Hebrew Scriptures link marital sexuality with procreation but not to the extent some assert. The first creation account includes the charge to be fruitful and multiply, regarded by the rabbis as the first commandment, to be fulfilled through remarriage or polygamy if a woman failed to produce (Mishnah Yebamoth 6.6). But the second creation account gives priority to companionship and unity, and it doesn't mention procreation until after departure from Eden. Later in Genesis, Jacob toils for his beloved Rachel and is disappointed to discover that Leah has been substituted as his bride—the two women personifying the conflict between personal love and cultural conventions (Gen. 29:16–31). Elkanah puts this in concrete terms when he comforts his childless wife Hannah with the touching reminder that he is dearer to her "than ten sons" (1 Sam. 1:8). Although the cultures of the Hebrew Bible expect procreation and see it as a blessing, marital sexuality is shown to be loving, unitive, and generative even when it is not procreative.

Jesus offers minimal teaching on marriage, stressing fidelity and permanence, overturning the law's provision for divorce (Deut. 24:1) as an accommodation to hard-hearted men (Matt. 19:8; Mark 10:5). He omits the commandment to be fruitful and multiply in his commentary on marriage as it was "in the beginning," stressing only the unitive aspect by which the couple become one (Matt. 19:4–8). He roots the call to fidelity and permanence in the creation accounts, but he does not attribute virtue to marriage in itself—an earthly phenomenon unknown to those worthy of the age to come, who cannot die anymore (Luke 20:34–36). He makes no mention of procreation in connection with marriage, though the absence of marriage in the resurrection may reflect it is no longer needed, any more than other goods of marriage—union and fellowship—fulfilled in that age where all are one. He commends celibacy as a sign of that age, for those able to receive it (Matt. 19:11).

Paul (or those writing in his name) offer the most extended reflections on marital sexuality. In 1 Corinthians 7, he frames it principally as a guard against commercial or casual sexuality, by providing couples an outlet for their sexual drives: the "remedy for fornication"—as Anglican liturgies would later frame it. On a positive note, he stresses mutuality: each member of the couple belongs to the other. He commends abstinence for times of prayer but only for short periods, lest couples lose control and fall into infidelities. Like Jesus, he commends celibacy to those who can accept it. Also like Jesus, he does not mention procreation beyond acknowledging the existence of children.

Ephesians, attributed to Paul, blends practical advice and theological perspective. It fleshes out the spiritual nature of mutuality by taking the relationship of Christ with the church as a template for couples' lives. This model is adapted from Hebrew tradition, analogizing the love of spouses with the love of God for God's People. The analogy is often negative (Jer. 3; Eze. 1, 16, 23 and Hosea 2 and 3), but Paul echoes the Song of Songs to emphasize the positive, using marriage in parallel to the *mystery* of the many becoming one in the church, Christ's body. His message is not, "If you want to know something about Christ and the church, look to marriage," but "If you want to know how to make your marriage work, look to Christ's work with the church."

Ephesians arises from and is addressed to a context and culture in which the secondary status of women was normative and so is problematical in an era affirming the equality of the sexes. However, within its context it points toward greater mutuality. The author stresses a paschal notion, the man giving himself for the woman (rather than the conventional call for the woman to surrender to the man) in 5:25. This echoes 1 Corinthians 7:4, where mutual authority is explicit, each spouse holding "authority" over the body of the other. Despite the language of male headship in Ephesians, the *role* of the head is not domination, but care, redemption, and self-giving—a self-sacrificing Christ gives his life for the church, echoing the Johannine inversion of master and servant as he did on the night before he suffered (John 13:13–15).

Ephesians explicitly echoes the primal story of Genesis 2. Just as Adam recognizes *himself* in Eve—"of his flesh and of his bones" (some manuscripts of Ephesians 5:30 include the phrase)—the church shares a corporeal identity with Christ. Christ loves the church, which is his body—formed in Baptism and fed in Eucharist, "holy by cleansing . . . with the washing of water by the word" and "nourished" by Christ (5:25–26, 29). The church is both Bride of Christ and Body of Christ, bridging the biblical canon between the imagery of Genesis and Revelation.

Ephesians picks up on Jesus's summary, "Love your neighbor as yourself" (5:33), and provides an answer to "Who is my neighbor?" by expanding the standard sequence of household moral advice as in Colossians 3. In the church (the "assembly" that by its nature unifies the plural), Jew and Gentile are made one out of two through the flesh and blood of Christ (2:13–14, 21–22), and husbands and wives, parents and children, slaves and masters are all neighbors to each other. The message for loving all of these neighbors is the same Jesus gave: "Go and do likewise."

This brings us to Galatians and its glimpse of a life in Christ in which these social distinctions disappear and in which "there is no longer male and female." "Male and female" recalls the language of Genesis 1:27, and indicates replacement of marriage in the original creation by the "new creation" in the body of Christ (6:15) in which marriage is transcended. Many translations, including some early versions (Palestinian and Latin) read "male *nor* female" to parallel the categories Jew/Greek and slave/free. This suggests an end to sex or gender itself, as well as sexuality and marriage. In either case, this realizes the "as-if" world of 1 Corinthians 7:29–31, an anticipation of life in the world to come here and now. Galatians also notes that "the fruit of the spirit is love, joy, peace, patience, kindness, generosity, faithfulness, gentleness, and self-control. There is no law against such things" (5:22–23). It is not marriage as institution, but the living, faithful, and mindful enactment of loving disciplines, rights, and responsibilities that reflect and embody the love of Christ for his body, the church.

Tradition and Marital Sexuality

When we turn to the tradition, the Christian rule for many years was "no sexuality outside of marriage"—but there were also restrictions on when, how, and why a married (or betrothed) couple might enjoy sexuality—if they enjoyed it at all! Asceticism and natural law restricted marital sexuality to the purposes and goods laid out by Augustine of Hippo and articulated by Thomas Aquinas: procreation, society, and sacrament. The scholastic emphasis was on procreation, though the latter two hold primacy in the teaching of Jesus and Paul. Aquinas held that procreation derives from our animal nature; shared life from the human nature; and the sacrament from the couple as believers. This suggests that "the primary end of specifically *human* marriage is dictated by a man's generically *animal* nature."[12] It is hard to see why human relationship should be subordinated to biological function.

In keeping with this focus on procreation, tradition early commended abstinence when procreation was impossible, and deprecated non-procreative sexuality. Augustine of Hippo reflected that "between husband and wife, the better they are, the earlier they have begun by mutual consent to abstain from sexual intercourse," but while he admired the asceticism of his forebears, he realized that times were changing, and allowed that intimacy "beyond the necessity of begetting is pardonable" though marred with concupiscence (*The Good of Marriage* 3,12). He condemned non-procreative sexuality and held "the use of any part of a wife's body not suited to generation to be wicked" (*On Marriage and Concupiscence* 2.20).

49

Still even conjugal sexuality with the intent to have children was ruled out during certain times and seasons.[13] Roman Catholic teaching continues to oppose any active form of contraception. However, in an evolution from earlier tradition, current Roman Catholic teaching permits non-procreative sexuality in foreplay (or afterplay) so long as it takes place in the context of sexuality that is "ordered" to procreation.[14]

Anglicans rang their own changes on the tradition at the Reformation. The first Anglican marriage liturgy (1549) cites traditional goods of marriage inherited from Rome, but reorders and rethinks them: first is procreation, care, and upbringing of children, but second is Paul's safety valve (a "remedy against sin, and to avoid fornication"), and third is mutual society, help and comfort. Anglicans did not call marriage a sacrament, as it "lacks any visible sign or ceremony ordained of God" (Articles of Religion XXV), but the preface to the marriage rite cites the symbolic function of representing the union of Christ and the church. The liturgy recognized marriage served other purposes even when the first could not be fulfilled, by directing the omission of the prayer for procreation "where the Woman is past childbirth."

Through the course of the last and into the current century, Anglicans and Episcopalians continued to downplay the procreative purpose of marital sexuality. While two worldwide gatherings of Anglican bishops (the Lambeth Conferences of 1908 and 1920) and the Episcopal House of Bishops (1925) condemned contraception, the 1958 Lambeth Conference bishops assigned parents "responsibility for deciding the number and frequency of children" (Resolution 115). By 1968 the shift was complete, as the

Lambeth gathering formally disagreed with the Roman Catholic position of *Humanae Vitae,* "that all methods of conception control other than abstinence from sexual intercourse or its confinement to the periods of infecundity are contrary to the 'order established by God'" (Resolution 22).

Changes in the liturgy echoed this evolution. Although the first American Book of Common Prayer (1785/89) took an Enlightenment approach and dispensed with *all* the traditional ends or goods of marriage, in 1979 all but the "remedy for sin" were restored, though reordered. "Mutual joy"—with its sexual implications—is stated as God's first intent. We need not adopt an ethic of hedonism, however, since pleasure has its place and the stress is on mutuality, and reflects an altruistic ethic where sex is understood not as the "use" of another, but as the gift of oneself to another. The greatest pleasure in sexual relations is giving pleasure to one's spouse, and when each make this gift to the other, as the poet Auden said, "all their occasions shall dance for joy."

This joy is followed by the social good of help and comfort. Procreation follows, "when it is God's will." This rearrangement reflects the rational (and biblical) view that procreation is a blessing that comes to some marriages when possible, and that it should follow *from* the mutual joy of the couple, and be surrounded by it: there is more to life than birth. So the 1979 liturgy continues by stressing not just the birth of children, but "their nurture in the knowledge and love of the Lord." This opens the institution of marriage to the wider community in which "it takes a village"—in this case the church as the body of Christ—to raise a child. This is the highest form of Gospel altruism—in which the church as body of Christ gives of itself for the good of the youngest and weakest of its members. It also takes account of the powerful biblical imagery of how adoption, rather than procreation, figures as dominant in the Pauline writings and the life of Jesus (as Virgin-born and foster-fathered).

The summer of 2015 saw further changes, as marriage equality became a reality in state and church. The U.S. Supreme Court recognized the legal status of same-sex marriages, and The Episcopal Church amended its canons and began the constitutional process for providing liturgies to celebrate such marriages. These changes grew out of a recognition that the core of marriage is not in the sex-difference of the couple but in the form of their commitment to the marriage vows by which their lives are joined together. After all, couples can and do have sexual relations without being married—but harking back to the biblical purpose Paul articulated (that marriage is a remedy for and preventative of casual sexuality) the church affirmed a belief that sexuality is best exercised in the context of a relationship that is permanent, faithful, mutual, and loving—which is what the marriage vows highlight. Such relationships—regardless of the sexes of the couple—can model themselves on the template of Christ's love for the church, his body and spouse.

Discerning the Body
Body of Christ and Spouse of Christ

The church is the household of God—with many rooms through which the people of God move. Sometimes the journey is strange; people we never expected show up not as guests but as family. To return to the analogy of the body, there are, as Paul said, many organs and members, but they cooperate with each other as the body "builds itself up in love" (Eph. 4:16). How can we as individuals, and the church as a whole, make use of the tensions—personal, social, and ecclesiastical—that have arisen over issues of sex and sexuality? One way is to appreciate that the body is not the same throughout; different organs have different functions. So, too, the church can function even when different parts of it work differently, through the love that binds the church together.

Some claim we must "do the theology" before making any changes in church discipline. The historical truth is that the church does not "do the theology" before acting; the action is part of the theology as much as breathing is as part of life—you are doing both now, theologically as you reflect, and biologically as you breathe. Theology does not appear spontaneously in books on a shelf—it forms in human lives and is enacted there, just as the Word of God, immanent in Scripture, took living flesh and walked among us in Jesus Christ. The church was content not to have a spelled-out theology of the Trinity for over two centuries. A fleshed-out theology of the Eucharist had to wait almost a millennium, and even then the debates continued with sharp differences of opinion. If the church can be of no or different minds on fundamental doctrines, it should be able to deal with new or different understandings of sex and sexuality.

Theology of the hard-bound sort is always after-the-fact, work of explanation and understanding, not of action; it looks back on the actions before it can understand them, just as the apostles only understood the Scriptures about Jesus's passion and resurrection after the fact. As you, a member of the church, reflect on the testimony of Scripture and of ages past, you will be doing theology. You will be guided both by the moral compass and the evidence of human lives, including your own, for it is only in lives that we can see the virtues Jesus valued, or not at all. One of the fruits of this journey is that together we may come to grasp more about sex and sexuality than we understood before, even learning from the least likely quarters. It would not be the first time that the stone rejected by the builders proved to be what was needed to hold the building up.

Meanwhile, sex and sexuality may be so simple a child can understand:

Child: Daddy, why do people get married?
Father: So they can have children.
Child: But Uncle Jim and Aunt Barbara are married,
        and they don't have any children.
Father: Well, they love each other very much.
Child: Oh, that's OK then.

Could it be as simple as that? Augustine of Hippo would have recognized this conclusion; even Aquinas in his better moments would have smiled. More importantly, so would Jesus.

Notes

1 *Laws of Ecclesiastical Polity* III.8.
2 The Outline of the Faith, Book of Common Prayer, 845.
3 James F. Childress and John Macquarrie, eds., *The Westminster Dictionary of Christian Ethics* (Philadelphia: The Westminster Press, 1986), entry on "Natural Law."
4 Maimonides, *Mishneh Torah*, Issurei Biah 21:8.
5 Thomas C. Caramagno, *Irreconcilable Differences* (Westport, CT: Praeger, 2002), 31.
6 James A. Brundage, *Law, Sex and Christian Society in Medieval Europe* (Chicago: University of Chicago Press, 1987), 54.
7 See, for example, a study from the *International Journal of Urology*, March 1999, 130–34.
8 Much has been written on the subject. My own *Reasonable and Holy: Engaging Same-Sexuality*, was published by Seabury Press in 2009.
9 See Jacob Milgrom's analysis in *Leviticus 17–22* (New York: Doubleday, 2000), 1785–90.
10 Marvin Pope, *Song of Songs* (New York: Doubleday, 1977), 644–45.
11 This section draws on the "Biblical and Theological Framework for Thinking about Marriage" in the Report of the Task Force on the Study of Marriage, published in *Reports to The General Convention of The Episcopal Church* (New York: The General Convention, 2015), 483–604.

12 Michael G. Lawler, *Marriage and Sacrament: A Theology of Christian Marriage* (Collegeville, MN: The Liturgical Press, 1993), 61.

13 For a helpful flow-chart see Brundage, *Law, Sex and Christian Society*, 162.

14 Christopher West, *Good News about Sex and Marriage*, rev. ed. (Cincinnati: Servant/Franciscan Media, 2004), 91–95.

Printed in the USA
CPSIA information can be obtained
at www.ICGtesting.com
JSHW012056140824
68134JS00035B/3482

9 780898 691306